FOOTPATH WALKS IN

SURREY

David Weller

COUNTRYSIDE BOOKS

NEWBURY BERKSHIRE

First published 2009
© David Weller 2009

COUNTRYSIDE BOOKS
3 Catherine Road
Newbury, Berkshire

To view our complete range of books,
please visit us at
www.countrysidebooks.co.uk

ISBN: 978 1 84674 117 3

*To my wife Marilyn for her
invaluable help and support*

Photographs and maps by the author

Designed by Peter Davies, Nautilus Design
Typeset by CJWT Solutions, St Helens
Produced through MRM Associates Ltd., Reading
Printed in Thailand

CONTENTS

FOOTPATHS FOR FITNESS

FOOTPATHS FOR FITNESS **GRADE 3 – HIKE**

Introduction

We all know that exercise is good for you and the fact that you bought this book indicates that you would like to achieve a higher level of fitness, or you may wish to shed a few pounds in weight. An alternative could have been to join a fashionable health club where the fee gives you access to all sorts of ingenious equipment designed to hone your muscles and burn off calories while all the time looking at a blank wall.

Well, there are certainly no blank walls here. These pleasurable routes pass through some of the best countryside and prettiest villages that Surrey can offer.

Walking is one of the most accessible and enjoyable forms of exercise; it will burn off calories and help you to maintain a healthy weight; boost your metabolism, increase energy levels, improve circulation and lower blood pressure as well as being great fun – the benefits are endless!

Each route includes an estimated calorie burn and although it is not an exact science, it gives an idea of expected calorie loss with my figures representing three body weights, 9 stone/12 stone/15 stone. At salient points around each circuit I have given a guide time so that you can measure your pace against mine, although I am no Olympian. The best guide is to walk fast enough to raise your heart rate and body temperature while still being able to hold a conversation.

I have graded the walks as follows, Grade 1 – Stroll, Grade 2 – Stride and Grade 3 – Hike. If you are new to the wonderful world of countryside walks then begin with the Grade 1 circuits of between 1¾ and 2¾ miles which can be completed in 1 hour or less before moving on to the Grade 2 circuits of between 4 and 6¾ miles that take between 1¼ and 2 hours. Finally, with increased fitness and muscle tone, tackle the Grade 3 routes of 7¾ and 8 miles that should take between 2¼ to 3 hours to complete.

All the routes are circular and can be walked during any season. For footwear I recommend you wear good walking boots as these give grip when mud is encountered and offer ankle support on uneven ground. A road map will get you to the starting point of each walk while my sketch maps and instructions are sufficiently detailed to lead you around the circuit, although I have recommended the relevant Ordnance Survey map as they give a better overview of the area.

A place of refreshment for each route is suggested and while in most cases these are pubs, I am not recommending you undo the good work that your exertions have brought. I find a small haversack containing a bottle of water or a flask of coffee and a light snack sufficient.

Enjoy your healthy walking!

David Weller

Publisher's Note

We hope that you obtain considerable enjoyment from this book; great care has been taken in its preparation. Although at the time of publication all routes followed public rights of way or permitted paths, diversion orders can be made and permissions withdrawn.

We cannot, of course, be held responsible for such diversion orders and any inaccuracies in the text which result from these or any other changes to the routes nor any damage which might result from walkers trespassing on private property. We are anxious though that all details covering the walks are kept up to date and would therefore welcome information from readers which would be relevant to future editions.

The simple sketch maps that accompany the walks in this book are based on notes made by the author whilst checking out the routes on the ground. They are designed to show you how to reach the start, to point out the main features of the overall circuit and they contain a progression of numbers that relate to the paragraphs of the text.

However, for the benefit of a proper map, we do recommend that you purchase the relevant Ordnance Survey sheet covering your walk. The Ordnance Survey maps are widely available, especially through booksellers and local newsagents.

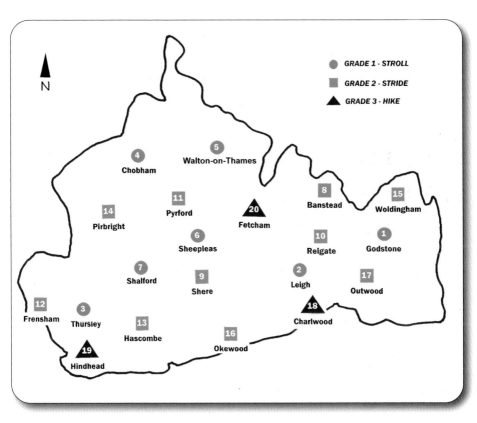

GRADE 1 - STROLL
GRADE 2 - STRIDE
GRADE 3 - HIKE

N

4 Chobham
5 Walton-on-Thames
11 Pyrford
14 Pirbright
20 Fetcham
8 Banstead
15 Woldingham
6 Sheepleas
10 Reigate
1 Godstone
7 Shalford
9 Shere
2 Leigh
17 Outwood
12 Frensham
3 Thursley
13 Hascombe
16 Okewood
18 Charlwood
19 Hindhead

Area map showing location of the walks

1 Godstone
Sunken Lanes and Field Paths

■ *A quiet sunken lane along the way* ■

This short introductory circuit** never strays far from habitation as it leads you around the lovely old village of Godstone and encourages you to stretch your legs a little and burn off a few calories. It also offers you the opportunity of measuring your level of fitness against my guide times. The circuit begins beside the pretty village pond and follows a quiet residential road before passing along the north bank of Bay Pond, a nature reserve, to reach a quiet lane. Turning south here brings us to Church Town,

8

that consists of no more than a few old houses clustered around St Nicholas church. A quiet sunken country lane leads to a couple of easy field paths that all too soon bring you back to Godstone's scenic pond.

1 Cross the road to the 16th-century **White Hart pub** and go left along the pavement passing the front of the pub. Pass the post office and when opposite a road named **Needles Bank**, turn right on a footpath that brings you to a residential road. Follow the road when it bends right and soon turn right into **Riders Way** and at its end, go left on a signed footpath. Now follow this path as it traces the bank of **Bay Pond** before passing between fields and ending at a country lane.
Distance: 0.65 mile. **Guide time:** *12 minutes.*

2 Turn right along the lane and soon pass **St Nicholas church** and a cluster of fine old houses. Parts of the church date from the 12th century while **Church End** and **Church House** are from the 17th and 18th centuries respectively. Next to the church are the beautiful **St Mary's Chapel and Almshouses** dating from 1872 which were built by a grieving mother in remembrance of her beloved daughter.

3 Pass this glorious setting and, after 60 yards, turn right into **Bulbeggars Lane**, where a short rise will increase your pulse rate slightly before the lane descends to meet a T-junction. Here go diagonally right along a short hedge-lined lane to meet a T-junction. Cross to the pavement opposite and turn left

GRADE: 1
ESTIMATED CALORIE BURN: 174/231/277

Distance: 1¾ miles.
Guide time: 35 minutes
Gradient: Lightly undulating
Number of stiles: 0
Underfoot: Most of the route is along hard surfaces and the remainder is generally mud free.
Starting point: Free car park by Godstone village pond. GR 350515
How to get there: Godstone is 1 mile south of junction 6 of the M25. The car park is opposite the White Hart pub in the centre of the village.
OS Map: Landranger 187, Dorking & Reigate
Refreshments: The White Hart opposite the car park or the Old Forge Café a few yards north.

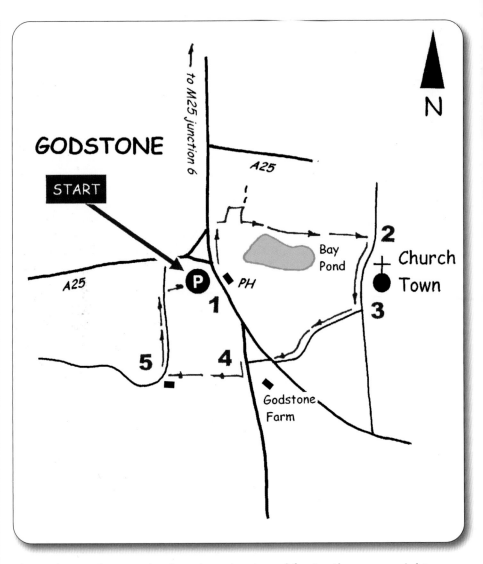

GODSTONE

START

to M25 junction 6

A25

A25

P

PH

1

Bay Pond

2 ✝ Church
● Town

3

5

4

Godstone Farm

N

along the road to reach a brook and a signed footpath on your right.
Distance: 1.24 miles. **Guide time:** *23 minutes.*

4 Follow the footpath alongside the brook and soon continue along the right side of a field. At its end, cross a planked bridge and press on along the right side of the next field to meet a tarmac path which you follow, passing close to a bungalow, before reaching a lane. Opposite are the indistinct

■ *Pretty almshouses in Church Town* ■

remains of **Ivy Mill** and the dam that held back the millpond until a heavy storm in 1909, when the dam burst signalling the end of the milling. The millpond was finally drained and filled in during 1947 and all that remains of the mill race is the brook that you followed earlier.

5 Turn right along the rising lane passing the end of **Ivy Mill Close** and Godstone village school to reach the village green where a right turn along a level tarmac path leads you back to the village pond and the end of this easy short stroll, which I hope will signal the start of your fitness regime. **Distance:** *1.75 miles.* **Guide time:** *35 minutes.*

Hopefully you finished this pleasant stroll close to my guide time and are encouraged enough to achieve greater fitness and tackle the slightly longer circuits in this section.

11

Scenic Fields and Pretty Hedgerows

■ *Pretty hedgerows line the route* ■

This easy field walk is glorious when the wayside flowers are in bloom and the hedgerows are alive with birdsong. This level part of the Surrey Weald below the North Downs offers the walker an opportunity to burn off a few calories while soaking up the far-reaching views. Beginning by the village green at Leigh (pronounced Lye), the route immediately immerses itself in the countryside as it crosses a patchwork of pretty fields in this part of the Weald. The wild flowers and rose-bedecked hedgerows are a great feature of this circuit and are at their very best during spring and early summer. Although there are a large number of stiles along the route, they are all fairly low and easily climbed.

1 From the lay-by, walk along the road away from the village green and at a bend, turn right through a kissing gate. Now go diagonally across a large arable field on a well-trodden path to its far corner. Bear right here alongside a second field and in 90 yards turn left over a plank bridge and stile. Go ahead through a field towards a house and cross a stile to reach a road.

2 Cross the road to a farm track opposite and press along it passing through a gate. When the track goes left, keep ahead on a fenced chalky track between fields and when this forks left, remain ahead along the left side of a meadow. Cross a plank bridge and a stile at the end of the meadow and continue along a hedge through the next meadow. Cross a double stile at the end of this meadow to enter a field with a byre ahead of you. *Distance: 0.85 mile.* **Guide time:** *15 minutes.*

3 Turn right here and follow the hedgerow on your right. Cross a stile and press on to enter woodland that is resplendent with bluebells in spring. Exit the woodland and press on ahead to a stile by a garden fence. Here follow a fenced path to soon meet with a road. Cross the road to a signed path opposite and continue ahead alongside a field. Cross a stile and turn

GRADE: 1
ESTIMATED CALORIE BURN: 356/410/454

Distance: 2¼ miles
Guide time: 42 minutes
Gradient: Level
Number of stiles: 19
Underfoot: Can be muddy during winter
Starting point: St Bartholomew's church beside the village green, Leigh. GR 224469
How to get there: Leigh is 3 miles south of Betchworth. Turn south off the A25 at a roundabout midway between Reigate and Dorking. Enter Betchworth and follow the signs to Leigh and park in a lay-by near St Bartholomew's church.
OS Map: Landranger 187, Dorking & Reigate
Refreshments: The Plough public house beside the village green

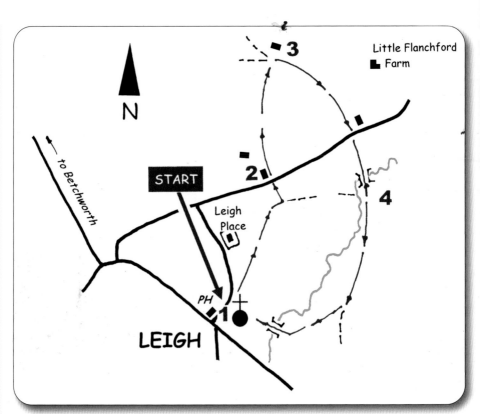

■ *Superb field paths are a feature of the circuit* ■

■ *St Bartholomew's church* ■

diagonally right across a corner of a meadow and continue over a small footbridge over a brook.

4 Go over the centre of a small meadow, cross a stile ahead of you and continue alongside a hedgerow. After 150 yards when the hedgerow bends right, maintain direction ahead over the centre of an arable field on a well-trodden path. At the far side of the field cross a stile and continue with a hedgerow to your right. At the end of this field the path divides and our way is now diagonally half right to a stile in the distant field edge. Cross the stile and go right on a fenced path and cross a small bridge over a stream. Continue through the centre of a meadow, cross a stile and press on along a fenced path to reach the graveyard of **St Bartholomew's church**, where you should pass the church to meet the lay-by and the end of this pretty walk.

Distance: *2.25 miles.* **Guide time:** *42 minutes.*

Thursley Bog and Common

A Naturalist's Paradise

FOOTPATH
FOR FITNE

■ *The circuit begins by following boarded walkways through the bog* ■

This **fascinating walk** is through one of the largest fragments of mire and wet heath in southern England. It is at its best during the summer months. Beginning beside the Moat, a beautiful lake and ideal picnic spot, the route follows boarded walkways that lead you between bog pools patrolled by dragonflies during summer, while on the fringes are marsh orchids and sundew, Britain's only insectivorous plant. After leaving the wetland pools, the circuit continues through the dry parts of the heath as it makes its way over **Thursley Common** where there is a chance of spotting a rare bird or two. A devastating arson attack in July 2006 affected 400 acres of the heath but fortunately nature is a master at healing itself and it is recovering well.

Walk to the shore of the **Moat** and follow the bank leftwards. The path soon bends right and brings you to a small junction of paths; turn left here and head away from the lake. In 60 yards at a wide crossing track by a National Nature Reserve sign, go ahead to join a boarded walkway that will now lead you through the bog. During early summer the mire is dotted with marsh orchids and sundew, while the fluffy white heads of cotton grass can be seen en masse. Press on until a path is met on your right.

Turn right here and soon pass by an informative dragonfly identification board. Remain on the path as it passes through a small area of woodland, before continuing along another boarded walkway followed by a well-trodden path. After bending left, the path meets a T-junction with a broad track.

Turn left at this T-junction and continue along the sandy track as it now leads you through the dry parts of **Thursley Common**. This area is often

GRADE: 1
ESTIMATED CALORIE BURN: 189/250/300

Distance: 2½ miles
Guide time: 43 minutes
Gradient: Level
Number of stiles: 0
Underfoot: Boarded walkways and sandy paths that are easier walked after rain.
Starting point: The Moat car park. GR 899416
How to get there: From the A3 south of Guildford, follow the B3001 to reach Elstead. Turn left at the village green and the Moat car park will be found on your left in 1¼ miles.
OS Map: Landranger 186, Aldershot & Guildford
Refreshments: The Woolpack pub by Elstead village green.

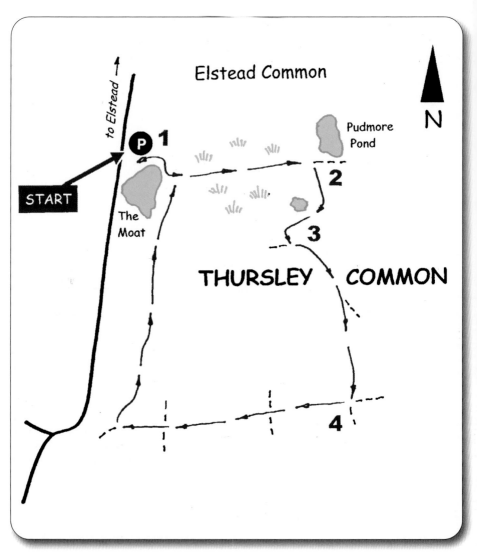

frequented by rare birds including the Dartford warbler and nightjar. When the track divides by a Heath Trail sign, ignore the left fork and continue ahead. Pass a barrier and, after 50 yards, meet a wide crossing track. **Distance:** *1.16 miles.* **Guide time:** *21 minutes.*

4 Turn right at this crossing track and ignore paths to left and right. In ½ mile and after a slight downward slope, look out for a signed bridleway on your

■ *The Moat makes a perfect picnic spot* ■

right which you should now follow. Remain on this wide sandy track until you finally reach the National Nature Reserve sign passed earlier. Here you should turn left and retrace your steps back around the end of the **Moat** to rejoin the car park and complete this interesting walk.
Distance: *2.5 miles.* **Guide time:** *43 minutes.*

Chobham Common
An Ancient Landscape

■ *A lovely track across Albury Bottom* ■

This easy-to-follow walk leads you through the ancient landscape of a part of Chobham Common, a National Nature Reserve recognized throughout Europe for its diversity of wildlife – some rare. The common is home to the Dartford warbler, the hobby and woodlark, as well as a host of rare plants including the marsh gentian. The route begins by following a track across Albury Bottom where traces of prehistoric man have been found; it was these early farmers who first cleared the forest and made this place so unique. After traversing the wilder parts of the common the route follows a track through woodland that all too soon brings you to the end of the walk.

1) Leave the car park on a wide track opposite the entrance and soon ignore a path on your left. After 100 yards take a right-hand fork and now follow this track as it passes through the wilds of **Albury Bottom** and heads towards a line of power cables in the distance. Ignore side paths. When nearing the power cables the track forks, 20 yards before a directional post and a single pine tree. Fork left here to meet a wide crossing track within yards.
*Distance: 0.81 mile. **Guide time:** 14 minutes.*

2) Turn left along this wide track and ignore another in 10 yards that forks right towards the cables. Keep ahead now on the track that remains parallel to the line of pylons and ignore side paths. The turning point comes when the track reaches woodland and when wooden rails on either side can be seen 20 yards ahead of you.
*Distance: 1.82 miles. **Guide time:** 30 minutes.*

3) Turn left here on a signed bridleway that follows the woodland edge before continuing between the trees. Again ignore side paths and remain on the

GRADE: 1
ESTIMATED CALORIE BURN: 190/250/300

Distance: 2¾ miles
Guide time: 45 minutes
Gradient: Level
Number of stiles: 0
Underfoot: Sandy tracks but some mud in section 3 during winter.
Starting point: Longcross car park at the junction of Staple Hill and Longcross Road. GR 979651
How to get there: From Chobham High Street, go north along Windsor Road (B383) for 1¼ miles before forking right into Staple Hill. Longcross car park will be found on your right at the junction with Longcross Road (B386) in 1¼ miles.
OS Map: Landranger 176, West London.
Refreshments: Various eateries and coffee shops in Chobham.

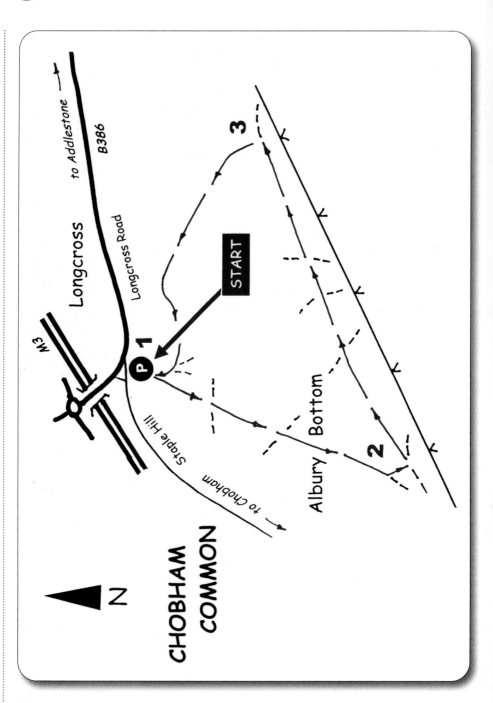

■ Shady woodland near the end of the circuit ■

main track until, after going over a small rise, the track ends at a T-junction. Here turn right and keep right when a path enters from the left. Soon the track is joined by the outward route and you should remain ahead to rejoin the car park in 100 yards.

Distance: *2.75 miles.* **Guide time:** *45 minutes.*

5 Walton-on-Thames
Desborough Island Delight

FOOTPAT
FOR FITN

■ *The quiet path around Desborough Island* ■

This delightful circuit is along the bank of the river Thames in this northernmost part of Surrey. Much of the route is around Desborough Island that was formed during the 1930s when the Desborough Channel was cut, not only to improve the flow of the Thames, but also to shorten the then still working waterway by 1 mile. Almost the entire route offers the walker lovely views of the river where pleasure craft ply the waters and rowers from single skulls to full rowing eights hone their skills. After circling the island that offers a degree of remoteness, the way returns along the pleasurable and popular towpath.

1 Cross the road from the car park and turn left along the towpath of the **river Thames**. Remain on this path until a bridge is reached where you should now go up steps to reach a lane. Turn right here and cross the bridge over the **Desborough Channel** and continue along this quiet lane. At a left bend beside a charming Victorian industrial building, continue ahead on a smaller track.

2 At a sharp bend in the track, keep ahead on a way-marked footpath that remains close to the riverbank. This pleasant wooded path continues to follow the river and you should ignore a couple of paths to your left. Finally the path turns left by a coal duty post and brings you to **Point Meadow**, a lovely open grassy area. Maintain your original direction now with a hedgerow close on your right to reach the end of the island, where you will see a grand white house on the opposite bank.
Distance: 1.42 miles. **Guide time:** 25 minutes.

3 Continue to follow this lovely path as it bends left and press on along the water's edge. Soon the path divides. Follow the path closest to the water's edge and later, when the path swings left away from the river by a steel

GRADE: 1
ESTIMATED CALORIE BURN: 210/278/333

Distance: 2¾ miles
Guide time: 50 minutes
Gradient: Level
Number of stiles: 0
Underfoot: Generally mud free
Starting point: Cowey Sale car park, beside Walton Lane a few yards from Walton Bridge. GR 092664
How to get there: From the centre of Walton-on-Thames, follow signs to Walton Bridge and turn left into Walton Lane just before crossing the bridge. The car park is a few yards ahead to your left.
OS Map: Landranger 176, West London
Refreshments: The Riverside Café beside Walton Bridge.

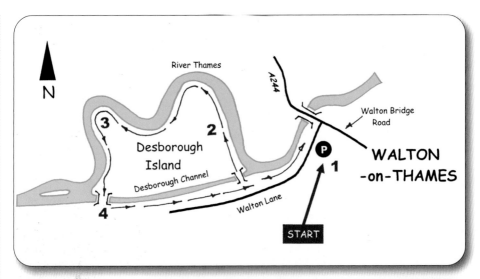

■ *Plenty of water traffic will be seen along the route* ■

■ *A narrowboat exiting Desborough Channel* ■

post, follow it up a slope to meet a road bridge over the **Desborough Channel**.
Distance: *1.78 miles.* **Guide time:** *32 minutes.*

4 Go over the bridge and down steps on the right to rejoin the towpath. Turn to the right passing under the bridge. Now with a good footpath underfoot you can really stride out and in almost no time at all pass under the first bridge you crossed and continue on to the car park and the end of this great little circuit.
Distance: *2.75 miles.* **Guide time:** *50 minutes.*

6 The Sheepleas
Charming Glades and Dells

FOOTPATH
FOR FITNE

■ *A wonderful woodland glade* ■

This **beautiful circuit** leads you through the woodland of The Sheepleas; a part of the Surrey Hills Area of Outstanding Natural Beauty, where a wonderful mixture of habitats supports a good diversity of wildlife and so is quite rightly designated as a Site of Special Scientific Interest. The way passes through woodland glades that are carpeted by cowslips in spring, while orchids, marjoram, eyebright and wild strawberry come to the fore a little later attracting many species of butterfly, thereby making this circuit a delight as well as a good chance to burn off a few calories.

1 Leave the car park through a gap in the railings beside a Surrey Wildlife Trust information board opposite the entrance. Keep ahead when tracks join from both sides and go left in 20 yards at a fork. Continue over a crossing track and soon pass the side of a woodland clearing and picnic area to meet a brick and flint viewpoint erected to celebrate the new millennium. Press on ahead down a grassy path that leads to another running along the foot of a shallow valley.

2 Turn left along this path and remain in the valley, soon passing through woodland and over a crossing track to reach a large woodland clearing. Continue ahead, pass a seat and go through another patch of woodland to reach a second clearing. Both clearings contain superb displays of cowslips in early May while orchids dot the whole area in June, but no matter how numerous the wild flowers are, please do not pick them. The path continues along the left edge and passes through a gate where you should press on ahead on a broad cart track beside a field. After passing **St Mary's church** our way meets with the busy A246.
Distance: 0.94 miles. *Guide time:* 17 minutes.

GRADE: 1
ESTIMATED CALORIE BURN: 244/292/350

Distance: 2¾ miles
Guide time: 49 minutes
Gradient: Rolling downland with an easy rise of 130 ft.
Number of stiles: 0
Underfoot: Generally mud free
Starting point: Shere Road car park, The Sheepleas. GR 084514
How to get there: Shere Road is off the A246 Leatherhead to Guildford road. At a small roundabout at West Horsley, 1 mile west of the tight S-bend at East Horsley, turn south into Shere Road to reach the car park on the left after ½ mile.
OS Map: Landranger 187, Dorking & Reigate
Refreshments: The nearest is the Barley Mow pub in West Horsley 1 mile north of the small roundabout, but this circuit has picnic written all over it!

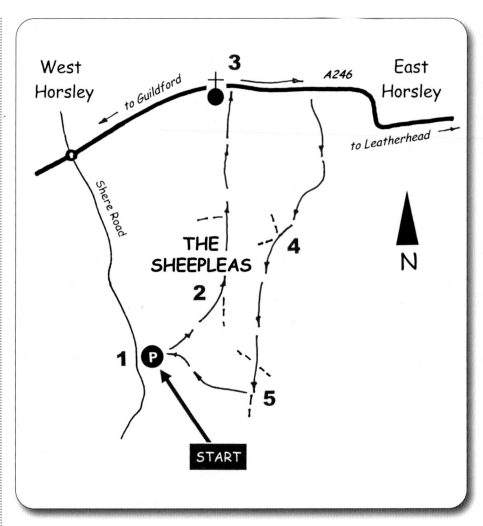

3 Cross the road to the pavement opposite and turn right alongside this unavoidable short stretch of road. Pass a house on your right and after 30 yards, turn right on a signed bridleway along a cart track where the quietness is soon restored. Remain on this peaceful track as it leads you through woodland.

4 At a junction of paths by the end of a field seen through trees on your right, turn left on a signed bridleway. For the next ½ mile the circuit gains height quite easily and will raise your pulse rate and knock off a few extra calories.

■ *Cowslips aplenty!* ■

Keep ahead at a large junction of tracks by a vehicle barrier and a handily placed seat. **Deadly nightshade grows beside this path, so if you are with children be aware that the enticing black shiny cherry-like fruits produced in autumn are extremely poisonous – four being enough to kill a child!** This area of forest suffered total devastation during the great storm of October 1987 but, as can be seen, it is recovering well. Finally at the top of the rise, a signed bridleway is met on your right with a field visible through the trees.
Distance: *2.15 miles.* **Guide time:** *39 minutes.*

5 Turn right onto this bridleway and ignore a gate on your left. At a seat by a path joining from the left, remain on the wider track as it bends right and goes downhill. At a junction of paths, go left on a path signed to **Shere Road** car park and in 20 yards fork right to rejoin the car park and bring this exquisite walk to an end.
Distance: *2.75 miles.* **Guide time:** *49 minutes.*

7 Shalford

The Path of Ancient Man

■ The Pilgrim's Way ■

This scenic walk circles an area of forest below Pewley Down known as the Chantries. It is along easily-followed tracks and field paths that give the walker some of the best views that Surrey can offer. The circuit begins along an ancient track that Victorian mapmakers romantically named as the Pilgrim's Way, although it is more likely to be of Neolithic origin. The track offers you the chance of really striding out and flexing your leg muscles while enjoying the scenery. At the turning point, the path leads you southward through woodland to meet an open hillside with truly breathtaking views. Soon the way joins a super field path that brings you easily to the end of this very good walk.

1 Walk towards a white house called **Chantry Cottage** and continue on a track to the left of it. Now follow this wide track and, at the entrance to **South Warren Farm**, ignore a track forking right into the forest and remain ahead. After the track narrows and passes between fields it meets with a junction of paths, here keep ahead on the signed **North Downs Way path**. The turning point comes at a house and country lane 30 yards ahead of you.
Distance: 1.10 miles. *Guide time:* 21 minutes

2 Turn right here through woodland and in 40 yards keep left at a fork, ignore side paths and soon exit the woodland beside a water tank to meet with an open hillside used as a scout camp. Press on ahead alongside the woodland and pass a hut and a couple of brick toilet blocks. At the end of the clearing that forms the scout camp, continue through a tree line, enter a second

GRADE: 1
ESTIMATED CALORIE BURN: 304/390/460

Distance: 2¾ miles
Guide time: 55 minutes
Gradient: Gently undulating with one short steep descent at point 3.
Number of stiles: 4
Underfoot: Generally dry but some mud in winter
Starting point: Car park off Pilgrim's Way, Shalford. GR 003483
How to get there: From the centre of Guildford, take the A281 south towards Shalford for ½ mile before turning east into Pilgrim's Way. After ¼ mile, at a left bend, fork right on a track to find the car park.
OS Map: Landranger 186, Aldershot & Guildford
Refreshments: The Seahorse pub on the A281 in Shalford

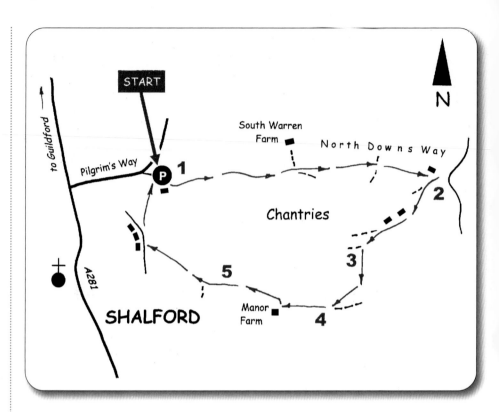

The magnificent view at point 3 of the walk

■ *The path at Manor Farm* ■

open space and in 20 yards fork left on an indistinct grassy path that continues along the edge of the escarpment.

3 When a hedgerow soon crosses the path by a marker post, turn left on a downhill path beside it and pass through scrub to meet a stile at a field edge. Cross the stile and go to the right over the field on a well trodden path to cross a stile at the far side.
Distance: 1.72 miles. **Guide Time:** *35 minutes.*

4 Now turn right along a well-used track. Ignore a path to your left in 35 yards. At the garden gate of **Manor Farm**, go to the right over a stile before continuing your original direction along a hedgerow. This level path gives you a great opportunity to really stride out as you head for the spire of **St Mary's church** at **Shalford**.

5 Remain on the path when it leaves the shelter of the hedgerow and bends right. Cross a stile at the end of the field to meet a residential road. Turn right here and in 40 yards fork right on a footpath that continues behind gardens to bring you back to **Chantry Cottage**, the car park and the end of this super walk.
Distance: 2.75 miles. **Guide time:** *55 minutes.*

I hope you enjoyed my Grade 1 walks and are encouraged enough to progress on to my Grade 2 routes that are slightly longer, but with your increased fitness they will be easily managed.

8 Banstead
A Woodland Wonderland

■ *The wonderful track through Perrotts Wood Nature Reserve* ■

This good circuit leads you through Banstead Wood where majestic beech trees form a wonderful canopy overhead, giving a cathedral-like quality to the woodland, while at the same time offering welcome shade on the hottest of days. After passing Perrotts Farm, the way follows a cart track between open fields and soon descends into Chipstead Bottom where it continues through Chiphouse Wood, a local nature reserve alive with bird song. The route soon climbs out of the valley and rejoins Banstead Wood where a welcome downhill track leads back to the car park to complete this excellent fitness-building circuit.

1 Leave the car park via a kissing gate opposite the car park exit. Go uphill passing a line of yew trees and keep ahead at a marker post. After 50 yards pass through a second kissing gate to enter **Banstead Wood**. The track now forks and here you should keep left and continue up a steep, fairly energetic but mercifully short uphill path to meet a track joining from the right by a thoughtfully placed seat. Turn right along this wide level track and now ignore all side paths and tracks.

2 Eventually the track goes down a slope and bends right to meet with a junction of tracks with the buildings of **Park Farm** seen to your right. Turn left here on a slowly rising wide stony track that passes through **Perrotts Wood** nature reserve where there is every chance of spotting a woodpecker or two, or if you are lucky, a deer. The track ends at a T-junction at the top of the rise with farm buildings ahead. Turn left here on a narrower path that winds its way between the trees before forking. Keep to the right fork and remain parallel to the farm buildings to join a wider path entering from the left. Go right along this path to meet and pass through a kissing gate by the buildings of **Perrotts Farm**.

3 Turn left and pass between a barn and a cottage and with the climb now over, fill your lungs with what the antiquary John Aubrey described as

GRADE: 2
ESTIMATED CALORIE BURN: 425/563/675

Distance: 4 miles
Guide time: 1 hour 15 minutes
Gradient: Undulating, with two not-too-difficult, pulse-raising hills.
Number of stiles: 0
Underfoot: One path in point 4 can be muddy in winter or after prolonged rain, otherwise mud free.
Starting point: Banstead Wood car park off Holly Lane, Banstead. GR 273583
How to get there: From the roundabout at the western end of Banstead High Street, go south on Bolters Lane (B2217) and soon continue ahead along Holly Lane (B2219) for 2½ miles to meet the car park just before the junction with Outwood Lane (B2032).
OS Map: Landranger 187, Dorking & Reigate
Refreshments: Plenty of coffee shops and cafés in Banstead High Street.

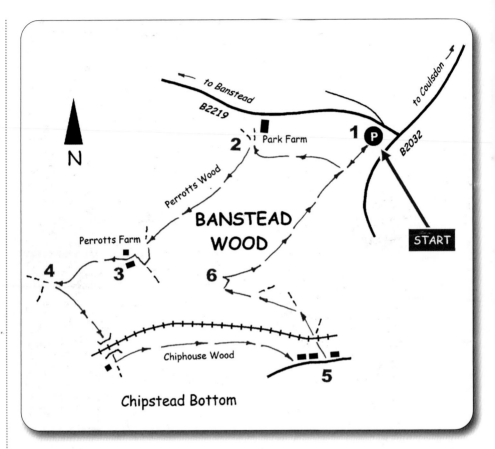

Banstead's '... *wholesome air, formerly much prescribed by the London Physicians to their patients, as the Ultimum Refugium'*. Now stride out along the farm track to the songs of unseen skylarks, but look out for a signed bridleway on your left at a right-hand bend after a downhill slope – there are two and ours is the first.
Distance: *1.52 miles.* **Guide time:** *28 minutes.*

4 Turn sharp left through a gate and continue on the downhill bridleway between fields and eventually pass under a railway bridge. Some 50 yards after the bridge turn left through a kissing gate and continue on a level path through **Chiphouse Wood** nature reserve. During early April the woodland floor is carpeted by the pretty white flowers of the wood anemone while later in the month the bluebells are unsurpassed. Go through a second kissing gate; soon ignore a left turn under the railway and

■ *A part of the route follows this quiet farm track* ■

press on to meet with a road. Turn left along the road for a short distance and look out for an easily missed signed public footpath on your left beside **Rosemere Cottage**.
Distance: *2.71 miles.* **Guide time:** *47 minutes.*

5 Turn left here for the second of our two climbs. Pass through a gate taking heed of the Stop, Look and Listen sign before embarking across the railway track. Press on at the far side and ignore a right turn in 10 yards. When a fork is soon reached, keep left to meet a crossing path with a kissing gate beyond. Pass through this gate and continue uphill over downland, passing

a tempting seat, before going through another kissing gate to re-enter **Banstead Wood**. Press on to meet a path in 15 yards where you should turn left and continue along a line of mature beech trees to reach a T-junction. Here turn right and in 6 yards go left to meet the top of the hill and another T-junction in 15 yards.
Distance: 3.19 miles. **Guide time:** 1 hour.

6 Turn right here and really get into your stride as you remain on this wonderful track, happy in the thought that it is all downhill from here. Soon the track joins our outward path where you should now retrace your steps to the car park and the end of this invigorating circuit.
Distance: 4 miles. **Guide time:** 1 hour 15 minutes.

I hope that you found my guide time achievable in this, the first of my Grade 2 circuits.

■ *Bluebells colour the woodland floor during late April* ■

■ *Near the start of the walk* ■

This really good fitness-building walk begins beside the Silent Pool, a well-known Surrey beauty spot, and crosses fields to reach a second – the pretty village of Shere that writers have described as the jewel in Surrey's crown. After passing through the village, the way heads over open fields where the panoramic views are quite breathtaking and, almost unnoticeably, the route climbs steadily to its highest point in the woodland of Albury Park where birdsong resounds from every tree. Descending to the open parkland below, the path passes by a disused but still consecrated Saxon church that is worth a visit. After following a lovely driveway out of the park the route all too soon ends.

1 Walk through the car park exit and go left along a pavement for 100 yards before turning right over the dual carriageway and continuing along the left side of a road named **Sherbourne**. In 250 yards turn left on a signed uphill track to reach a field. Pass through a kissing gate and maintain direction across the field and go over a stile at its end. Now continue ahead on a well-worn path through woodland before passing through another kissing gate and continuing over a large grassy area, crossing a drive along the way. Press on through a ribbon of woodland to meet a quiet country lane.

2 Ignore a footpath opposite, turn right along the lane and pass by pretty **Chantry Lane Cottage** to meet the **Tilling Bourne stream**. Cross a footbridge and turn immediately left through **Vicky's Gate** to enter a meadow. Continue alongside the stream, pass through another gate, and remain ahead on an unmade track. When this becomes hard-surfaced, keep

GRADE: 2
ESTIMATED CALORIE BURN: 472/618/738

Distance: 4¼ miles
Guide time: 1 hour 18 minutes
Gradient: Two hills, neither difficult.
Number of stiles: 2
Underfoot: Generally mud free.
Starting point: Silent Pool car park: GR 059484
How to get there: The Silent Pool car park is beside the A25 almost 2 miles west of Gomshall and is well signed.
OS Map: Landranger 187, Dorking & Reigate
Refreshments: The circuit passes close to the Lucky Duck Tearooms in Middle Street, Shere.

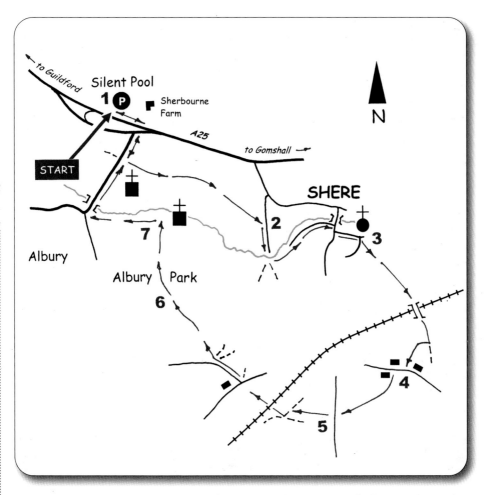

ahead and soon pass the **Old Jail** to reach the centre of **Shere** where the stream passes under **Middle Street**. A few yards to your left is the **Lucky Duck Tearoom**. Our way lies diagonally right along **Church Lane**, where you pass by the war memorial to meet the junction with **Church Hill**. *Distance: 1.27 miles. Guide time: 25 minutes.*

3 Fork right here through a gate and continue up an easy calorie-burning hill on a fenced path to reach a large field and a junction of paths. Go ahead on a rising path to the top of the field where the view back to **Shere** and beyond is beautiful. Follow a fenced path, cross a railway bridge and at the end of the field on your right, turn right on a bridleway that soon leads you

■ *Tudor cottages line the streets of Shere* ■

between gardens to meet a road by the entrance to **Burrows Lea Farmhouse**.

4 Turn right along the road for 25 yards before going left on a signed footpath. Pass by a gate to be met by a wonderful panorama over Surrey. Keep to the path as it bends right and remains close to a large

garden before narrowing between fences as it passes through fields and ends at a road.
Distance: *2.35 miles.* **Guide time:** *43 minutes.*

Cross the road and continue ahead on a well-trodden path through woodland to meet a T-junction by a water utility borehole where you should turn left to meet a lane in 50 yards. Now go right along the lane, pass a line of cottages and when it bends left, keep ahead through a gate and cross a railway line, bearing in mind the Stop, Look and Listen sign. Ignore a bridleway on your right in 10 yards and remain ahead to reach a road junction in 350 yards. Go ahead along **Park Road** and when it bends left by **South Lodge**, ignore a bridleway and kissing gate to your right and fork right on a track beside the house. Pass through a gate and in 50 yards fork left on a well-marked path which you should now follow through magnificent woodland where the highest point of the circuit is reached.

The path now descends to the parkland below. Just before this is met, ignore a field gate to your left and fork right on a narrow path to exit the woodland via a kissing gate. Go diagonally right here and cross a drive in 30 yards where you keep ahead to soon meet a cart track with the Saxon church of **St Peter and St Paul** to your right.
Distance: *3.52 miles.* **Guide time:** *1 hour 4 minutes.*

The route from here is leftwards where within yards the main driveway is met and, with less than a mile to go, here is the chance to really lengthen your stride and make up for any time you may have lost. Follow the drive out of the parkland and turn right before bearing right alongside **Sherbourne** where you soon retrace your steps back to the car park and the end of this great walk.
Distance: *4.25 miles.* **Guide time:** *1 hour 18 minutes.*

10 Reigate Heath
The Windmill Church

■ *A quiet byway below Colley Hill* ■

This lovely route passes within half a mile of the old market town of Reigate, although once immersed in its rural charm you would never guess it. Soon after the start, the way heads along a quiet exclusive residential road to meet with a byway that brings you to the foot of the chalk escarpment of Colley Hill. The route now follows the romantically named and very ancient Pilgrim's Way along the foot of the hill before we meet up with a super bridleway that follows a ribbon of woodland between fields where the views are stunning. After crossing level fields the route climbs a knoll to pass Reigate's windmill church before soon bringing this great circuit to an end.

46

1 Walk along **Flanchford Road** and at its junction with the A25 turn right along the main road and pass the **Black Horse pub**. When a cluster of modern bungalows is reached, and number 71 in particular, cross the main road to an easily-missed footpath. Follow this footpath between gardens until it brings you to a road where you should press on ahead over a railway bridge. Keep ahead now as the road passes through a suburb of **Reigate**.

2 When the road dips and bends left, maintain direction ahead on a hard-surfaced byway where the superb scenery is set against the back-drop of **Colley Hill**. Fork left on the byway by a cottage and at a barrier ignore side paths and remain ahead to meet the **Pilgrim's Way** that joins from the right in 50 yards.
Distance: 1.43 miles. Guide time: 24 minutes.

3 Go ahead here and ignore a right turn in 45 yards. Now remain on this undulating path as it winds its way along the foot of **Colley Hill** with fields never far away to your left. At a fork by a post, and with another path to your left, continue ahead along the left fork. Soon pass by the end of a garden and climb steep curving steps that will raise your pulse rate a little. The path finally brings you to a barrier by a junction of paths.

4 Turn left here on a signed bridleway and continue through a ribbon of woodland between fields. For the next 2 miles the circuit is perfectly level and the good paths underfoot will enable you to raise your pace and burn

GRADE: 2
ESTIMATED CALORIE BURN: 368/488/585

Distance: 4½ miles
Guide time: 1 hour 19 minutes
Gradient: Undulating
Number of stiles: 1
Underfoot: Generally mud free but point 3 can be slippery in winter or after rain.
Starting point: Flanchford Road parking area. GR 238502.
How to get there: From Reigate High Street, follow the A25 west towards Dorking and in ½ mile turn left into Flanchford Road. The car parking area will be met after ¼ mile.
OS Map: Landranger 187, Dorking & Reigate
Refreshments: The Black Horse pub near the beginning of the circuit.

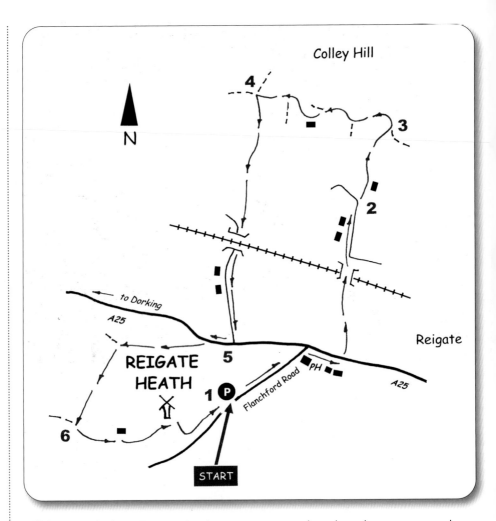

off extra calories. At a quiet lane, press on ahead and soon go under a railway bridge. After passing a scattering of splendid houses our way meets the A25.

Distance: *3.02 miles.* **Guide time:** *52 minutes.*

5 Turn right along the pavement beside the road until you are opposite a Mole Valley District Council 'Welcomes Careful Drivers' sign. Unfortunately the drivers are generally going too fast to read it, so take great care as you cross to the far side before going ahead to reach a signed public footpath in 12 yards. Continue along this narrow path and at its end cross a stile before

■ *Along the way* ■

pressing on ahead along a field edge to reach a fingerpost. Turn left at this post and follow the right-hand field edge until finally turning right through a gate and continuing on a cart track to meet a junction of tracks beside the cooling waters of the **Shag Brook**.

6 Turn left at this junction and follow a cart track signed **GW (Greensand Way)** through a field to meet **Ivy Cottage** beside the fairway of **Reigate Heath Golf Club**. Follow the **GW path** ahead over the fairway (check for flying golf balls from your right first) and press on uphill on a sandy path just to the right of the clubhouse. The post-mill behind the clubhouse was built in 1765 and has been used as a chapel since 1862, surprisingly it is big enough to seat a congregation of 50. Pass through a parking area and by a cottage before turning right on the downhill **GW path**. A few yards before meeting **Flanchford Road**, turn left on a bridleway that remains close to the road and follow this back to the parking area and the end of this good circuit. ***Distance:*** *4.5 miles.* ***Guide time:*** *1 hour 19 minutes.*

■ *Papercourt Lock on the Wey Navigation* ■

This is such a good circuit for building up your fitness because, apart from one short easy hill, the route is level which allows you to really swing your arms, flex your muscles and set a good pace. Within yards of the beginning, the way passes the site of Newark Mill, once Surrey's largest watermill now sadly gone, and soon continues alongside water meadows that contain the stark remains of Newark Priory. After a short climb up a knoll to reach Pyrford's ancient church, the circuit heads across Fox Hill where panoramic views are on offer. After passing through the outskirts of Old Woking the route meets the Wey Navigation where the pretty towpath is followed back to the car park.

1 Leave the car park at the end furthest from the entrance and continue alongside the road crossing two bridges. To your right here was the site of **Newark Mill** while a little further along the road you will notice the remains of **Newark Priory** in the water meadows. Press on along the pavement on the right-hand side of the road and, when that ends, continue along the left side. At a sharp right bend in the road, go ahead through trees up the only hill in the circuit to pass **Pyrford's ancient church**. Rejoin the road and press on by **Church Farm** to meet the top of the incline and a signed bridleway beside a house.
*Distance: 0.87 miles. **Guide time:** 15 minutes.*

2 Turn left and remain on this bridleway as it leads between fields before crossing a golf course. At a wide crossing track by a way marker, turn left on a tarmac drive lined by poplars. Soon go through a field gate and fork right passing to the right of a cottage at **Roundbridge Farm**.

3 At a junction of tracks turn right and in 15 yards go left on a signed footpath to cross a bridge. Now keep ahead on the footpath until it ends at an unmade track. Turn right on this track that soon becomes hard-surfaced and remain on it as it passes through a cluster of cottages before finally ending at a road.
*Distance: 2.63 miles. **Guide time:** 44 minutes.*

GRADE: 2
ESTIMATED CALORIE BURN: 335/444/532

Distance: 4¾ miles
Guide time: 1 hour 18 minutes
Gradient: Level apart from one short low hill
Number of stiles: 0
Underfoot: Mud-free in summer but point 4 can become waterlogged (but not impassable) during winter or after prolonged rain.
Starting point: Car park off Newark Lane. GR 039573
How to get there: From Ripley High Street, turn north on Newark Lane (B367) and 250 yards after passing the Seven Stars pub, turn left into an easily-missed car park. Ripley is off the A3 some 2 miles south of junction 10 of the M25.
OS Map: Landranger 186, Aldershot & Guildford
Refreshments: The Seven Stars pub nearby, or one of a variety of pubs in Ripley.

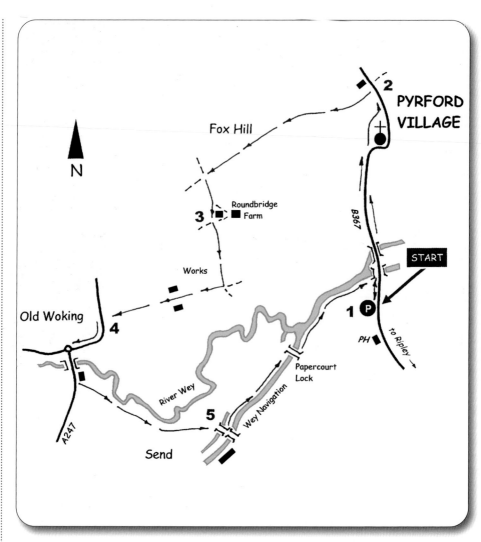

4 Cross the road and turn left along the pavement. Follow the road when it bends right and passes the **White Hart** public house to meet a mini roundabout. Turn left here on the A247, cross the **river Wey** and at the end of cottages on your left go left through a gate. Now cross a huge area of low lying grassland on an indistinct bridleway that at first follows a wire fence before later heading towards a distant factory. The bridleway finally brings you to a wooden bridge in front of the factory.

Distance: *3.71 miles.* **Guide time:** *1 hour 2 minutes.*

■ *Colourful narrowboats ply the waters throughout the summer* ■

5 Cross the bridge to meet the **Wey Navigation** but ignore a second bridge ahead of you. Turn left now along the towpath where you pass colourful narrowboats moored along the bank. Just after passing a lock-keeper's cottage at **Papercourt Lock**, turn right over a bridge before maintaining direction along the right-hand side of the navigation through fields. At a road, turn right on a path to rejoin the car park within a few yards where this good circuit ends.
Distance: *4.75 miles.* **Guide time:** *1 hour 18 minutes.*

12 *Frensham*
Surrey's Lake District

■ *Sail boats on Frensham Great Pond* ■

This **excellent circuit** takes in both Frensham Great and Little ponds. Although they look totally natural today, the ponds were actually created during the 13th century as fisheries for the Bishop of Winchester who often resided at nearby Farnham Castle. This good muscle-toning circuit begins by following the foreshore of Frensham Great Pond before heading across Frensham Common, a wonderful area of heather and pine, to reach Frensham Little Pond. After an easy climb over King's Ridge the way heads back to the shore of Frensham Great Pond where the circuit ends all too soon.

1 Exit the car park from the right-hand corner nearest the water's edge and follow a sandy path that remains close to the shoreline to meet a lane. Turn left along the lane for a short distance and left again on a lane by the **Frensham Pond Hotel**. After passing a sailing club, cross a stream and 10 yards later fork left on a path through woodland. When this divides by a marker post, follow the right fork to rejoin the road. Turn left along the road and 40 yards after passing the gateway to **Heather Warren**, swing left on a path through woodland that soon forks at a barrier. Here take the right fork to meet the A287 in 40 yards.

2 Go ahead over the road and continue on a wide sandy bridleway where you can really increase your pace. After climbing an easy pulse-raising rise and going down the other side, you meet a junction of paths. Here you should maintain direction ahead ignoring two paths to left and right. Soon after going around an S-bend a serene lake may be glimpsed through the trees in private grounds to your right. After passing a large house the bridleway divides and here you should take the right fork. Pass the entrance gates to **Grey Walls** to meet a lane in 40 yards.
Distance: 1.98 miles. *Guide time:* 34 minutes.

GRADE: 2
ESTIMATED CALORIE BURN: 396/525/630

Distance: 4¾ miles
Guide time: 1 hour 23 minutes
Gradient: Fairly level with an easy rise of 100 ft to the summit of King's Ridge.
Number of stiles: 0
Underfoot: Sandy tracks that are easiest walked after rain. Some mud in winter.
Starting point: Frensham Great Pond car park (open 9 am to 9 pm) for which a charge applies on summer Sundays and Bank Holidays. GR 844405
How to get there: From Farnham follow the A287 south for 3 miles to Frensham village. Pass the village green and school and 50 yards later turn right on a road signed to the car park which will be found on your left in ½ mile.
OS Map: Landranger 186, Aldershot & Guildford
Refreshments: There is a café bar in the information centre beside the car park during the summer.

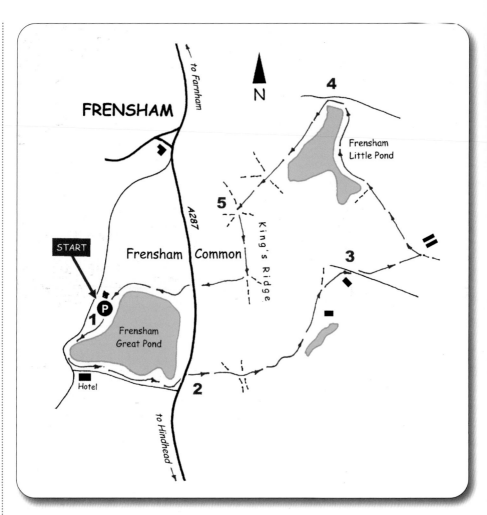

3 Turn right along the lane, cross a ford and 180 yards later fork left on a wide signed bridleway through pine trees. Follow the bridleway until it reaches a crossing track by a field with two Nissen huts ahead of you. Turn left here, pass between barriers and continue at a good rate along a narrow fenced path, but beware of exposed tree roots that conspire to trip you up. After passing a National Trust sign the path divides but both paths soon rejoin the main route and the shore of **Frensham Little Pond**. Continue around the end of the lake and cross a bridge over the outflow to reach a lane.

*Distance: 3.20 miles. **Guide time:** 54 minutes.*

■ *Frensham Great Pond* ■

4 Turn left along the lane and in 80 yards fork left by low metal railings. Keep left in 8 yards and cross a grassy area to meet a National Trust information board and a wide track. Turn left along this sandy track and follow it as it remains close to the shoreline. When the track leaves the shoreline behind, it meets with a large junction of tracks. Here ignore tracks to left and right and go ahead for 10 yards before taking a left fork that will lead you directly up the side of **King's Ridge**. A good test here is to get to the top without stopping.

5 A wide track is met at the summit and here you should follow it leftwards. Soon pass by a barrier to meet a large junction of paths in 50 yards. Ignore all side paths and press on along the top of the ridge for a further 350 yards where a smaller junction of paths by a directional post is met. Turn right here towards **Frensham Great Pond** that is now clearly in view. Pass a **King's Hill Barrows** information board and follow a narrow path downhill between gorse bushes to reach the A287. Cross the road by a bus stop, bear left and follow a sandy path to reach the shore of **Frensham Great Pond** where you continue ahead to meet the car park and the end of this exhilarating walk.
Distance: *4.75 miles.* **Guide time:** *1 hour 23 minutes.*

FOOTPATH
FOR FITNE

■ *The easy climb up Hascombe Hill* ■

An Arcadian retreat is how F.E. Green described Hascombe in his book entitled *The Surrey Hills*. Well, that was a century ago and not much has changed since then, although the village is not quite so remote nowadays. This good calorie-burning circuit begins in the centre of the village and after passing an attractive pond, the way climbs fairly easily over Hascombe Hill to meet a wonderful track with panoramic views. After following the foot of the hill awhile the route turns and heads west where it traverses the valley in which Hascombe sits and follows a quiet, exclusive private road before finally descending to the village where this good muscle-toning walk ends.

1 Walk back to the B2130 and turn right to meet the village spring within yards. Cross the road to a footpath opposite where you soon go over a brook. When the path ends at a T-junction with a bridleway, turn right to pass **Lower House** and meet a lane. Turn right along the lane where you will pass the rural charm of the village pond and rose-adorned cottages.

2 The lane ends at the **White Horse pub** and here you should pass the frontage before turning immediately left on a driveway signed as a bridleway. Remain on the drive as the surface deteriorates and pass the splendid Georgian façade of **Hascombe Place**. Continue ahead to the right of a bungalow where the bridleway now narrows and starts to climb between banks lined by trees. When a large meadow opens up on your left, look out for a path forking left that continues to climb the hill alongside the meadow. At the crest of the hill, ignore paths to left and right and re-join the bridleway a few yards to your right. Now follow the bridleway downhill until, 25 yards after passing a tennis court, a junction of tracks by a vehicle barrier is met.
Distance: *1.52 miles.* **Guide time:** *28 minutes.*

3 Turn left, pass the vehicle barrier and remain on this wide bridleway as it continues along the foot of the hill. Here you can set a good pace for 1 mile before the bridleway ends at a country lane.
Distance: *2.55 miles.* **Guide time:** *47 minutes.*

GRADE: 2
ESTIMATED CALORIE BURN: 510/675/810

Distance: 4¾ miles
Guide time: 1 hour 29 minutes
Gradient: Hilly, but not too demanding.
Number of stiles: 0
Underfoot: Some mud in winter or after prolonged rain.
Starting point: Mare Lane, Hascombe. GR 997398
How to get there: Hascombe is on the B2130, 3½ miles south-east of Godalming. When travelling from the Godalming direction, Mare Lane will be found on your right and signposted to the village hall. Park at the roadside.
OS Map: Landranger 186, Aldershot & Guildford
Refreshments: The White Horse pub is near the beginning of the circuit.

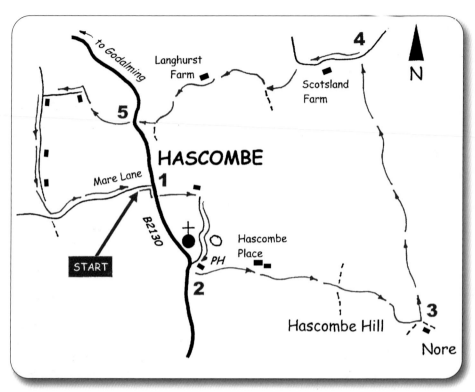

■ *Hascombe nestles in a sheltered valley* ■

■ *A far-flung view from the route* ■

4 Turn left along the lane and pass the exquisite buildings of **Scotsland Farm**. At the end of its walled garden go left on a signed bridleway that is also marked as the **Greensand Way** long-distance path. Keep on the track when it bends right and climbs a short hill to meet a T-junction at the top. Here leave the long-distance path by turning right on a descending bridleway. Soon the way traces the edge of rolling fields and passes **Langhurst Farm** that sits in its own small piece of Arcady. After passing a couple of large fields a directional post is met on a left bend. Turn right here and with a white house seen ahead of you, pass between paddocks to meet the B2130 at a blind bend.
Distance: *3.58 miles.* **Guide time:** *1 hour 6 minutes.*

5 Our way continues on the track opposite, alongside **Yew Tree Cottage**. *To safely cross the road, use your ears as much as your eyes to avoid approaching traffic.* Press on up the track that soon becomes quite steep, you may need to take a rest or two along the way – I did. Fortunately the track is short and levels out beside aptly-named **High Winkworth**, where it also meets a private road. Go left along the road and at a T-junction with another private road signed as a bridleway, go left along it where you can now pick up speed. After passing grandiose houses the tarmac surface ends and you should continue ahead through a gate to meet with **Mare Lane**. Turn left, and after descending between high banks and passing a cricket green, this great circuit soon ends.
Distance: *4.75 miles.* **Guide time:** *1 hour 29 minutes.*

14 Pirbright
Doctor Livingstone, I Presume

FOOTPATH
FOR FITN

■ *The walk starts beside Pirbright village pond* ■

This splendid woodland figure-of-eight walk features lovely tracks that allow you to keep up a steady pace without having to search for your footing. Soon after leaving Pirbright's pretty village green the way passes St Michael's churchyard, the last resting place of one of the most famous Victorian explorers – Sir Henry Morton Stanley. Soon the route explores quiet paths and tracks to the north-west of the village before swinging south on a fine bridleway between fields to reach the crossing point of the figure-of-eight route. After continuing through beech woodland where the canopy offers shade from the heat of the day, the way reaches Stanford Common from where it returns to Pirbright along pretty woodland paths and tracks.

1 Walk back to the A324 at **White Hart Corner**, cross to a service road opposite and turn right to soon meet **Church Lane**. Go left along the lane where you will soon notice the large Dartmoor granite gravestone marking **Stanley's grave** in the churchyard. The inscription 'Bula Matari' was the name given to him by his African porters and means 'rock breaker'. Press on along the lane and at the end of the churchyard turn right over a stream and continue on a woodland path until it ends at a road.

2 Turn left along the road and soon fork left into **West Heath**, signed as a bridleway. Pass a collection of houses of varying sizes and after rounding a bend, ignore **Thompsons Close** on your left and fork right to meet a T-junction with a lane. Turn right along the lane and soon turn left on a signed bridleway along the drive to **West Hall Farm**. Before reaching the house, the drive divides and here you should turn right and continue between barns before exiting the farm on a charming bridleway between fields.

GRADE: 2
ESTIMATED CALORIE BURN: 428/551/650

Distance: 5 miles
Guide time: 1 hour 26 minutes
Gradient: Level
Number of stiles: 5
Underfoot: Parts of section 4 can be muddy during winter or after prolonged rain.
Starting point: Beside the pond on Pirbright village green. GR 947559
How to get there: Pirbright is on the A324, 4 miles north-west of Guildford. When approaching from the Guildford direction, turn right at White Hart Corner, pass the White Hart pub and park in a lay-by beside the pond. Additional parking can be found further around the green.
OS Map: Landranger 186, Aldershot & Guildford
Refreshments: The Cricketers pub opposite the pond or the White Hart further along the road.

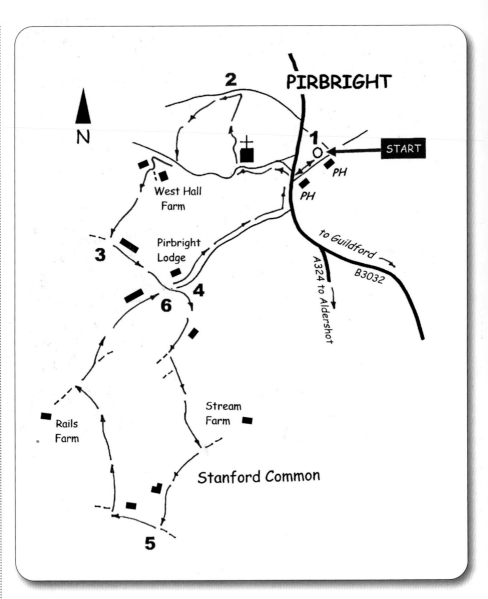

3 The bridleway ends at a T-junction and here you should turn left and soon pass by a large modern barn. Press on ahead on a narrower bridleway and 30 yards later meet with a junction of paths at the end of a garden. Go ahead here on a bridleway following power lines to meet with a drive. Bear right along the drive and maintain direction ahead when it is joined by

■ *Near Pirbright Lodge* ■

others, to reach the gateway of **Pirbright Lodge,** with a field visible ahead of you.

Distance: *1.78 miles.* **Guide time:** *34 minutes.*

4 Turn right here on a wide track alongside the field and at the end of the large garden of **Admiral's Walk**, turn left on a signed footpath. Ignore a path on your right and continue ahead through woodland. Pass an MOD sign and at the end of woodland cross a plank bridge over a stream and continue ahead over a grassy area. At the far side, cross a stile and continue through woodland that can be boggy in winter. Cross a stream and a stile to meet a T-junction in 30 yards. Go right on this bridleway and later pass

■ *Stanley's grave is marked by this huge granite stone* ■

the entrance of **Bourne House** where you go ahead along its drive to meet a T-junction with a military track.
*Distance: 2.96 miles. **Guide time:** 52 minutes.*

5 Turn right along the track, pass **Wood House** and then go right again at an MOD barrier. In 40 yards ignore a path to your left and continue ahead through a gate and along a pretty path through woodland. As you exit the woodland, cross two stiles in quick succession and continue between fields to a final stile to meet with a broad crossing track. Turn right here but soon look out for a fork 12 yards before the entranceway to **Rails Field**, a wood yard. Continue on this wide track as it follows power lines and passes a group of isolated houses to again reach the gateway to **Pirbright Lodge**.

6 Go ahead along **Mill Lane** where you can really speed up and burn off a few extra calories. The lane finally ends at the A324 where a left turn soon brings you to **White Hart Corner** where you will see the pond and the end of the circuit to your right.
*Distance: 5 miles. **Guide time:** 1 hour 26 minutes.*

15 Woldingham

Delightfully Different

FOOTPATHS
FOR FITNESS

■ *On the path to Woldingham* ■

This superb fitness-building circuit is fairly energetic, but well worth the effort. Beginning on top of the North Downs the route follows a section of the Vanguard Way long-distance path as it heads for Woldingham where the way passes along quiet roads lined by the sizeable mansions of the stockbroker belt. The turning point comes at Woldingham Garden Village and later the circuit passes by Woldingham's pretty village green to meet the open countryside once again, where a steady climb brings the walk to an end. The contrast between the rolling downs, the mansions, and the charm of the rose-bowered garden village makes this walk delightfully different.

1 Leave the car park via a tarmac path furthest from the entrance and at a road continue ahead for 50 yards to meet **Chalkpit Lane**. Turn left here on a drive alongside the unique brick wall of **Flint House**. The drive is also part of the **Vanguard Way** long-distance path as it heads for the coast. Ignore a left fork, press on ahead and when the tarmac ends, continue ahead on a cart track. After passing an isolated equestrian centre the track narrows, goes through woodland and brings you to open downland where you should go downhill on a narrow path to meet a road.
*Distance: 1.56 miles. **Guide time:** 26 minutes.*

2 Turn right along the road and in 200 yards, at **Blueberry House**, turn right over a stile hidden in a hedgerow. Go ahead alongside a meadow with a hedgerow on your right and cross a stile at the far side to meet a wide cart track. Here we leave the long-distance path by turning left along the track to pass farm buildings and re-join the road. Cross the road and continue along an unmade track opposite, When it soon ends at a T-junction, turn right and follow this glorious road dotted with mansions, until it ends at **Halliloo Valley Road**.

GRADE: 2
ESTIMATED CALORIE BURN: 654/837/986

Distance: 5½ miles
Guide time: 1 hour 40 minutes
Gradient: Hilly
Number of stiles: 8
Underfoot: Generally mud free
Starting point: Woldingham viewpoint car park. GR 385546
How to get there: Follow the B269 south from Warlingham for 3 miles. Pass by Botley Hill Farmhouse pub and turn right into The Ridge signed to Woldingham. Pass Chalkpit Lane and after 300 yards, look out for the car park on your left.
OS Map: Landranger 187, Dorking & Reigate
Refreshments: Simple refreshments from Woldingham village store along the route.

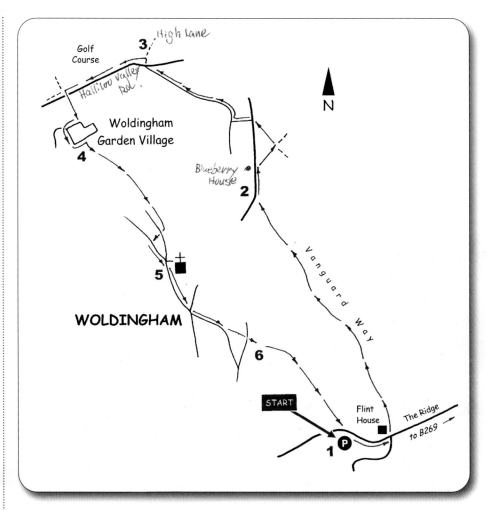

3 Cross the road and go ahead on a track named **High Lane**. After 40 yards turn left through a gate and continue on a footpath that follows the edge of a golf course. When the golf club entrance gates come into view ahead of you, and with the clubhouse at 2 o'clock on your right, go left up a short steep slope to a stile. Cross the road and a stile opposite and continue along the right side of a meadow. The meadow rises steeply so don't overdo it and take a rest if need be. Cross a stile at the top and press on between gardens to reach a quiet residential road in **Woldingham Garden Village**. Turn right along the road and at a junction go left along **Hilltop Walk**. At the top of a rise follow the road left and pass by the **Garden Village Hall**.

69

■ *The wonderful rolling downland* ■

Look out for a footpath on your right just before reaching a black-painted wooden bungalow that began life as an army hut. The village was originally built at the beginning of the First World War to house the Public Schools Battalion of the Middlesex Regiment but as casualties mounted it was converted into a convalescent camp.

4 The path leads between gardens before going down steps to meet a bridleway. Ignore the bridleway and continue ahead on the well-trodden path signed as the **Woldingham Millennium Walk**. After offering super views over the valley the path meets with an unmade road where you should

continue on the footpath opposite that soon meets a road. Turn left alongside the road to reach **St Paul's church**.
Distance: *4.13 miles.* *Guide time:* *1 hour 12 minutes.*

5 Continue along the left side of the road and follow **The Crescent** as it curves past the local shops, that include the village store, before re-joining the road. Pass the village hall to meet a road junction by the green. Go ahead here along **Upper Court Road** and 35 yards after passing **Sylvan Mount**, turn left on a downhill path. Cross a lane at the foot of the slope and continue ahead along unmade **Southview Road** to pass a house.

6 Ignore a bridleway on your right and press on along the signed footpath that begins to climb out of the valley. With fields and great views to your left, maintain your direction ahead until you finally reach a road where you will see the car park and the end of this great walk.
Distance: *5.5 miles.* *Guide time:* *1 hour 40 minutes.*

■ *Woldingham's pretty village green* ■

16 Okewood

In Remotest Surrey

FOOTPATH
FOR FITNE

■ *Roman Stane Street lies below this fine driveway to Ruckmans Farm* ■

This delightful walk passes through an area of Surrey that was once deep within the ancient Wealden forest and still remains a remote part of the county. Beginning beside one of Surrey's most isolated churches, the way soon follows a magnificent driveway that tops Roman Stane Street. After following super driveways and wonderful woodland tracks the circuit turns north to pass through the tiny hamlet of Paynes Green. The route back to Okewood continues along a quiet country lane and pretty cart tracks lined with summertime wild flowers. This circuit is especially good for fitness building as an excellent pace can easily be maintained along its entire length.

1 At the end of **Church Lane**, follow a tarmac drive that leads uphill to the church. Pass the door of the church and turn left on a tarmac path to meet the edge of the graveyard and a marker post beyond. Fork right at the post and in 15 yards turn right and continue on a path alongside a field. At the field end follow the path to the left where there are magnificent views towards **Leith Hill**. Cross a stile and go ahead for 20 yards before turning right beside a garden fence to meet a country lane. Go left along the lane, ignore a road to your right and press on, passing by the 17th-century **Punchbowl Inn**.

2 In 80 yards fork right on a narrow lane and when this bends left, turn right along the driveway to **Ruckmans Farm**, signed as a bridleway. This mounded drive tops **Roman Stane Street** that lies beneath. Keep ahead at a cluster of fine houses to meet a sharp left bend in the drive.

3 Follow the drive leftwards and when it bends right, continue ahead through a pedestrian gate on a marked bridleway. The track brings you to another pedestrian gate which you should pass through before continuing along a well-trodden path through mixed woodland, finally to meet with a lane where a right turn brings you to the A29.
*Distance: 2.43 miles. **Guide time:** 43 minutes.*

4 Cross the main road and go along **Weare Street** opposite and pass through the hamlet of **Paynes Green**. Remain on the road when it bends left and heads north. Pass a couple of modern cottages with idyllic woodland

GRADE: 2
ESTIMATED CALORIE BURN: 481/630/752

Distance: 6¼ miles
Guide time: 1 hour 47 minutes
Gradient: Fairly level
Number of stiles: 1
Underfoot: Some parts can be muddy in winter.
Starting point: Church Lane, Okewood. GR 128380
How to get there: From the A29, ¼ mile south of Ockley village, turn west into Cathill Lane and at its end go left on Standon Lane. Church Lane is ¾ mile on your left. Park on the roadside near the church.
OS Map: Landranger 187, Dorking & Reigate
Refreshments: The Punchbowl Inn is passed along the route.

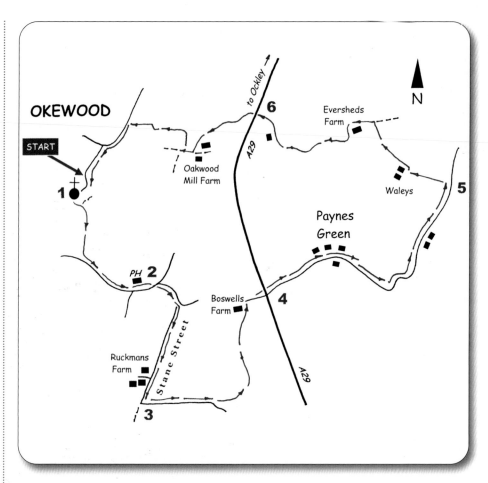

OKEWOOD

START

Oakwood
Mill Farm

to Ockley

A29

6

Eversheds
Farm

N

Waleys

5

Paynes
Green

PH 2

Boswells
Farm

4

Stane Street

Ruckmans
Farm

A29

3

dells as gardens and, after 400 yards, look out for a track named **Waleys** signed as a bridleway on your left.

*Distance: 3.7 miles. **Guide time:** 1 hour 3 minutes.*

5 Turn left along this track and at its end pass a field gate before turning immediately right and following a cart track that initially skirts a garden. After passing between fields the track ends at a T-junction with another beside a wildlife pond. Turn left here and keep to the track when it zigzags between the buildings of **Eversheds Farm**. After leaving the farmhouse behind, the track passes through a shallow valley and crosses a stream. On an upward slope, ignore a left fork and keep to the main track to pass a modern house and meet a junction of tracks beside barns. Turn right here

■ *The walk begins at one of the remotest churches in Surrey* ■

and when the track enters a garden, remain ahead to re-join the A29 in 20 yards.

Distance: *4.95 miles.* **Guide time:** *1 hour 25 minutes.*

6 Cross the main road and press on along the drive signed as a bridleway to **Middle Lodge**. At the gateway, continue on a bridleway to its left and pass through woodland. Pass through a pedestrian gate beside the yard of **Oakwood Mill Farm** and turn right to meet a field gate in 100 yards. Pass through this, ignore a left fork, and go ahead to meet a stile at a field edge. Ignore the stile, turn right through a pedestrian gate and continue on a narrow bridleway along the edge of woodland. Pass through a second gate and continue along a field edge. Look out for a third gate on your right which you should pass through before continuing on the bridleway to meet with **Standon Lane**. Turn left here to reach **Church Lane** to bring this super circuit to an end.

Distance: *6.25 miles.* **Guide time:** *1 hour 47 minutes.*

■ *The pretty Punchbowl Inn, passed on the circuit* ■

17 Outwood

A Wealden Treat

■ *Looking towards the North Downs* ■

This really is one of the best walks in the Surrey Weald, and what a way to burn off those unwanted calories along cart tracks with panoramic views and pretty hedgerows brimming with flora and fauna. Beginning on Outwood Common the way follows field paths with glorious views to bring you to a fine bridleway that leads you through woodland and up the only noticeable hill to reach Cuckseys Farm. As the route turns south it passes the grand buildings of South Park Farm and follows a track with fantastic views before reaching the ancient buildings of Lower South Park. The final leg of the circuit crosses more open fields with panoramic views and all too soon returns to Outwood Common.

1 Go back to the open common and bear left across the front of the **Chapter House** to reach a small lane. Turn left along the lane passing the **Windmill Garage** and later ignore a right fork. When the lane ends by a couple of cottages, press on ahead, cross a stile and continue over a small meadow to enter a large field. Now follow the right-hand field edge to meet and cross a stile at its far end to enter a field. Turn right here along the top edge of this and a second field to reach a third field.

2 The route now goes diagonally left across this field on a well-trodden path to reach and cross a stile in a hedgerow. Now maintain direction over the next two fields and stiles to meet with a road. Cross the road and turn left along it for 130 yards to reach a bridleway on your right by a bend. Go right here on a cart track and when it ends at a field, continue ahead alongside pretty woodland to finally reach a T-junction with a bridleway.
Distance: 1.76 miles. Guide time: 30 minutes.

3 Turn left here on a stony bridleway and remain on it when it later climbs a calorie-burning slope to reach an isolated house at its crest. Press on to reach **Cuckseys Farm** where you continue ahead on a concrete drive between the buildings to meet the farm gate, a couple of cottages and a driveway.
Distance: 2.77 miles. Guide time: 50 minutes.

GRADE: 2
ESTIMATED CALORIE BURN: 634/814/960

Distance: 6¾ miles
Guide time: 2 hours
Gradient: Gently undulating with one noticeable rise of 160 ft in point 3.
Number of stiles: 8
Underfoot: Some mud during winter or after prolonged rain.
Starting point: The National Trust car park on Outwood Common. GR 325455
How to get there: From the A25 at the centre of Bletchingley, go south along Outwood Lane to reach Outwood Common and its windmill in 3 miles. Turn right on a rough track opposite Gayhouse Lane to reach the car park.
OS Map: Landranger 187, Dorking & Reigate
Refreshments: The Bell Inn a few yards north of the windmill.

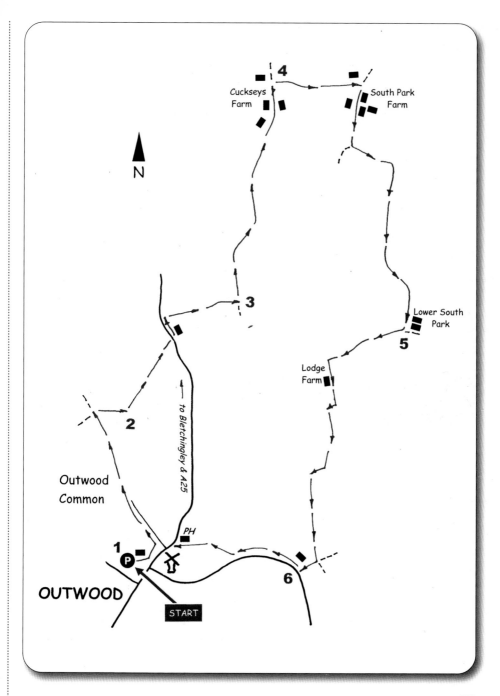

■ *Cart tracks with great views are a feature of this route* ■

4 Turn right here on a level bridleway along the tarmac drive where for the next mile or so you can really lengthen your stride and make excellent time. At a T-junction with another drive turn right, pass a pretty pond and continue between the buildings of **South Park Farm**. Remain on the driveway when it soon bends left and now follow it between fields for 1 mile as it gradually reduces in width to a bridleway before ending at a lane beside the exquisite buildings of **Lower South Park**.
Distance: 4.46 miles. **Guide time:** *1 hour 18 minutes.*

5 Turn right along this lane that serves a few scattered houses before ending at the gate of **Lodge Farm**. Turn left 3 yards before the gate on a signed

bridleway that continues beside a field and soon goes right to meet a farm track. Now turn left along the farm track where you can maintain a good pace while climbing gently as the track follows the edge of two large fields with panoramic views for almost 1 mile. After passing through scrub, our way meets a crossing track in woodland and here you should turn right to meet a road beside **Hornecourt Cottage**.
Distance: 5.94 miles: *Guide time:* 1 hour 46 minutes.

6) Turn right alongside the road and after rounding one left bend, but before a second, cross a stile in the hedgerow on your right and enter a field. Go diagonally left across the field to a stile hidden in a hedgerow at the left end of a tree line. Cross this stile and press on along the right-hand field edge, with **Outwood mill** ahead of you. At the beginning of a line of fir trees, cross a stile on your right that handily brings you to the car park of the **Bell Inn** (just remember those hard-earned burnt-off calories). Pass the pub to meet a road where turning left for a few yards brings you to **Outwood Common** and the end of this great walk.
Distance: 6.75 miles. *Guide time:* 2 hours.

Completing this circuit in around 2 hours indicates that you are more than ready to take on the last three hikes.

■ *Outwood's old windmill signals the end of the walk* ■

18 Charlwood
Treading the Border Path

■ *During September, the hedgerows brim with autumn fruits* ■

This route traces a section of the 150-mile-long Sussex Border Path that begins at Thorney Island in West Sussex and skirts Surrey before ending at Rye in East Sussex. After leaving the ancient village of Charlwood, the circuit crosses a patchwork of fields under the flight path of Gatwick Airport, which will be of interest to any planespotters. The route leaves the long-distance path when it turns north and continues on a fine bridleway through woodland and more fields to reach the hamlet of

Cudworth. The return leg to Charlwood takes in wide tracks, field paths and the glories of Glover's Wood – untouched since Saxon times – to complete this really good muscle-toning walk.

1 Continue westward along **The Street**, passing **Rosemary Lane** and the **Rising Sun** before forking left in 40 yards along a narrow road to reach the church. Follow a path to the left of the war memorial that goes through the graveyard. Pass the church and, after 40 yards, turn left over a stile and continue ahead through a meadow, across a brook and along a grassy path to climb a stile in 80 yards. Maintain your original direction with a hedgerow to your left and follow the path as it passes the rear of a garden. Cross a stile beside a field gate and another in 25 yards and press on ahead on a grassy path through the centre of a large field, then cross two stiles in quick succession at the far side. Press on ahead towards a large barn with a hedgerow on your right.

2 Continue on a path beside the barn and pass a cottage to reach a road. Ignore the road and turn left on a drive for 5 yards before going right over a stile. Continue alongside a hedgerow that separates you from the road to reach the entrance to **Russ Hill Farm** where you meet the road. Press on along the road until a stile is met immediately after passing **Russ Hill House**. Cross the stile and again follow the hedgerow that divides you from the road until you rejoin the road to pass **Russ Hill Hotel**.

3 Immediately after passing the hotel, cross a stile on the left to enter a corner

GRADE: 3
ESTIMATED CALORIE BURN: 910/1115/1280

Distance: 7¾ miles
Time: 2 hours 31 minutes
Gradient: Fairly level
Number of stiles: 28
Underfoot: Can be muddy in winter.
Starting point: The Street in Charlwood village centre. GR 242412
How to get there: Charlwood is 2½ miles west of the A217, 1 mile north of Gatwick Airport. Park on the roadside by the local shops in the village centre.
OS Map: Landranger 187, Dorking & Reigate
Refreshments: The Rising Sun in Charlwood

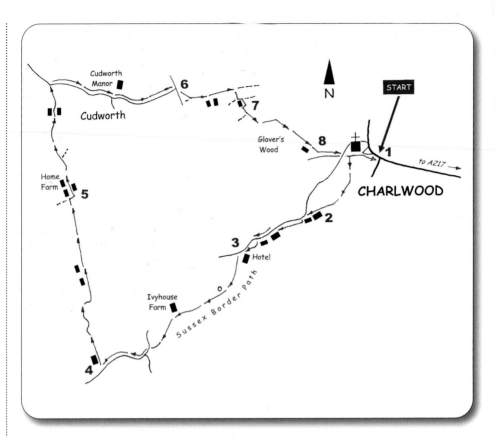

of Sussex. Now cross a field to a hedgerow opposite before turning right alongside it to reach the field end. Go ahead over a large field aiming 10 yards to the left of a dew pond surrounded by bushes. From here, continue ahead to a stile to the right of five oak trees in the distant hedgerow. Press on along a field edge and at a marker post, fork left and cross the field to another post under an oak tree. Now turn right alongside a hedgerow to meet a road and re-enter Surrey. Follow the road left, pass the end of **Orltons Lane** and press on until you reach a signed bridleway and a concrete drive on your right.
Distance: *2.73 miles.* **Guide time:** *56 minutes.*

4 Turn right along the drive, pass through a gate by stabling and follow the bridleway through woodland. When the bridleway emerges from the woodland, press on ahead with a hedgerow on your left. Pass through a ribbon of woodland and continue alongside another field with a hedgerow

■ *The route follows wonderful field paths* ■

on your left. Again pass through a ribbon of woodland to meet with a large arable field. Ignore a tempting cart track that forks left and continue ahead through the centre of the field where you should aim for a gap in the hedgerow opposite at around 1 o'clock. Now continue on the bridleway and pass through two pedestrian gates as you head towards the buildings of **Home Farm**. Pass a wildlife pond to reach a gravel area in front of the buildings and turn right to pass through a third gate to reach a track. **Distance:** *4.23 miles.* **Guide time:** *1 hour 27 minutes.*

5 Turn left along the track passing between farm buildings. When the track soon bends left, keep ahead through a fourth pedestrian gate and continue along the bridleway passing through a fifth gate. Remain ahead when the bridleway goes between farm buildings and passes **Green Lane Farm Cottage** that always has a wonderful display of summertime flowers. Press on along the farm drive where you can now set a good pace for the next 1¼ miles. At the farm gate turn right along a quiet lane and later

pass **Cudworth Manor** and a large tithe barn to eventually meet **Partridge Lane**.
*Distance: 5.91 miles. **Guide time:** 1 hour 55 minutes.*

6 Cross a stile opposite, enter a field and go diagonally right to its far corner and a stile. Continue through a ribbon of woodland and keep ahead along the right side of a field to enter woodland at its end. Go ahead over a brook and turn right to meet a track where you should now turn left. Pass farm buildings and 80 yards later look out for a signed path on your right. Cross a field to a stile hidden in the hedgerow opposite some 30 yards to the right of a white house.

7 Turn left along a drive and then right immediately after passing the house. Follow a way-marked path that skirts the garden and continue down the right side of a field soon ignoring a path on your right. At the field end, enter woodland and follow a well-trodden path that leads to another field. Maintain your original direction along the right-field-edge to its end and pass through a ribbon of woodland to reach a large field. Here go ahead to its bottom corner on a slope and follow a path, later passing **Brookside Cottage** to meet a road.

8 Turn left along the road and at its end go ahead on a footpath that leads to **Charlwood's church**, where you should re-trace your steps to meet the end of this good circuit.
*Distance: 7.75 miles. **Guide Time:** 2 hours 31 minutes.*

■ *The end of the route passes through ancient Glover's Wood* ■

19 Hindhead

The Land of the Broom-Squire

FOOTPATHS FOR FITNESS

■ *The panorama from the Devil's Punchbowl viewpoint* ■

This wonderful circuit with fabulous views is through an area made famous by Baring-Gould in his 1896 novel *The Broom-Squire* – a story of poor folk who scraped a living by making brooms from the brushwood below the Devil's Punchbowl. The circuit begins on the rim of the Devil's Punchbowl, one of Surrey's premier beauty spots before descending into secluded Highcomb Bottom as it heads for Thursley. After passing through the village the route crosses a part of Thursley Common from where it begins its return. A long steady climb that is none too taxing returns you to the rim of the Devil's Punchbowl and brings to an end this great fitness-building circuit.

1 From the National Trust car park, cross a grassy picnic area to meet a viewpoint and a well-trodden path a few yards beyond it. Turn right along this path and soon pass through a kissing gate. In 5 yards turn left on a wide stony downhill path through majestic woodland. Ignore any side paths and keep to the main track as it descends into **Highcomb Bottom**.

2 After finally exiting woodland and passing a line of old beech trees, now all joined together, turn right 50 yards later through a kissing gate. Now follow a path through a dell where you cross a bridge over a brook and continue ahead up a broader track. At a T-junction with a drive by a gate, go left and soon pass **Gnome Cottage** to meet with a cattle grid. Continue along this wonderful track for ¾ mile through scenery reminiscent of Scotland. To reinforce the Scottish theme, highland cattle often graze here for conservation purposes; although they have fearsome horns they are gentle creatures, but you should still not approach them. A fork is met on a left bend, with a field gate on either side and here you should follow the left fork. Soon cross a cattle grid and continue ahead to meet finally a small lane.
Distance: 2.33 miles. ***Guide time:*** *42 minutes.*

3 Go ahead along the lane where you can speed up and burn off extra calories. Remain on the lane as it passes a lovely cluster of houses around **St Michael and All Angels church** and later the ancient buildings of **Wheelers Farm** before it finally ends at a small triangular green. Keep to the left of the green to meet the main village street and cross the road to a

---

GRADE: 3
ESTIMATED CALORIE BURN: 792/1048/1258

Distance: 7¾ miles
Time: 2 hours 20 minutes
Gradient: Hilly but not too taxing
Number of stiles: 0
Underfoot: Generally mud free
Starting point: Devil's Punchbowl National Trust pay and display car park. GR 890357
How to get there: The car park is off the A3 just ¼ mile north of the Hindhead traffic lights.
OS Map: Landranger 186, Aldershot & Guildford
Refreshments: The Devil's Punchbowl Café beside the car park.

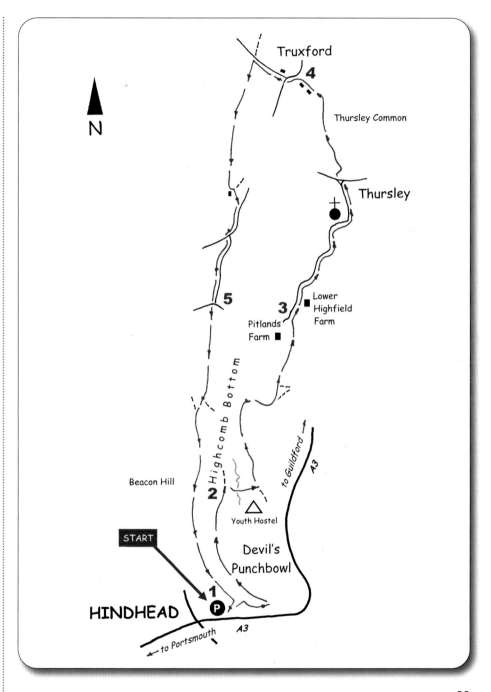

■ *Fantastic views are on offer on this hike* ■

bridleway opposite. The bridleway soon bends left in front of a double garage and narrows as it enters woodland and meets a junction of paths. Turn left here, go over a crossing track in 25 yards and continue over a corner of **Thursley Common**. Keep to the main track when the bridleway re-enters woodland and soon follows the edge of fields on your left. At the field end follow the bridleway left, pass a barn and later a house to meet with a road.

Distance: *4.02 miles.* **Guide Time:** *1 hour 10 minutes.*

4 Turn left along the road and in 90 yards turn right on a lane beside **Truxford Cottage**. Follow the lane until a wide crossing track is met near MOD warning signs. Go left along this track where you can again speed up – war games were being played out when I last came this way but that didn't stop me getting close to a grazing roe deer. At a sharp left bend, fork right on an uphill bridleway to soon meet a road. Turn right and pass a few well

appointed houses before turning left into **Sailors Lane** which you should follow until it ends at a T-junction with **Hyde Lane**.
Distance: *5.75 miles.* **Guide time:** *1 hour 41 minutes.*

Here go ahead on a bridleway that passes between high banks initially bordered by holly. After emerging from between the banks, there is a gate and you should remain ahead where the incline eases as you pass through open woodland. Keep ahead as the path follows the rim of the **Devil's Punchbowl** with panoramic views over **Highcomb Bottom**, where you can spot your earlier path below. Continue through a gate beside a cattle grid, go through a small parking area and fork left after passing a height barrier. Now continue along a well-trodden path until the viewpoint is met where you should turn right to reach the car park and the end of the exhilarating walk.
Distance: *7.75 miles.* **Guide time:** *2 hours 20 minutes.*

■ *Pretty cottages in Thursley* ■

FOOTPATH
FOR FITNE

■ *Stepping out on a field path* ■

This great circuit has the lot, easy stretches of level byway, a not-too-challenging rise of 360 ft to the top of the North Downs at Ranmore Common and a long downhill section that allows you to really stride out and make good time. Beginning on Fetcham Downs, this wonderful route leads you through tranquil and charming scenery where only a couple of isolated farms and cottages are passed along the way. The circuit passes through the wonderful parkland of Polesden Lacey where Sheridan, the 18th-century playwright, sought his rural idyll. The panoramic views, majestic woodland and wide tracks make this a not-to-be-missed calorie-burning and fitness-building opportunity.

1) Leave the car park via the vehicle entrance, turn right and in 50 yards go right again onto a public byway. Soon ignore a path forking off to the right and press on ahead. At a junction of tracks by the end of the field on your left, turn right on a bridleway and soon pass the uniquely named **Roaringhouse Farm**. Keep ahead now with woodland to your left and a field to the right. This section offers very easy walking and good time can be made.

2) A junction of tracks is met at the end of this field and here you should turn right, and right again in 15 yards on a bridleway. In 90 yards turn left on another bridleway and continue alongside woodland with open views to your left. Press on along the slowly rising bridleway ignoring side paths. After rising 130 ft the way meets with a radio mast on the crest of a hill near **Phoenice Farm**.
Distance: 1.66 miles. **Guide time:** *30 minutes*

3) As the bridleway descends into a valley it offers great views towards the wooded **North Downs ridge** at **Ranmore Common** topped by the spire of **St Bartholomew's church**. Finally pass through two gates to reach a lane where you continue ahead along the drive to **Bagden Farm**. Pass a house and 10 yards before a barn, turn right through a field gate, pass the front of the barn and go through a second field gate. Continue ahead through a field, keeping a bank to your right. Pass through a gate at the far side to meet a T-junction.
Distance: 2.42 miles. **Guide time:** *45 minutes.*

GRADE: 3
ESTIMATED CALORIE BURN: 850/1125/1350

Distance: 8 miles
Guide time: 2½ hours
Gradient: Undulating with one long rise of 360 ft.
Number of stiles: 0
Underfoot: Some mud in winter or after prolonged rain.
Starting point: Fetcham car park (free), Norbury Park. GR 151548
How to get there: The car park is off a roundabout at the top of Young Street (A246) 1½ miles south-west of Leatherhead town centre.
OS Map: Landranger 187, Dorking & Reigate
Refreshments: Bocketts Farm tea shop ¼ mile further along the car park entrance road. Free admission to the tea shop.

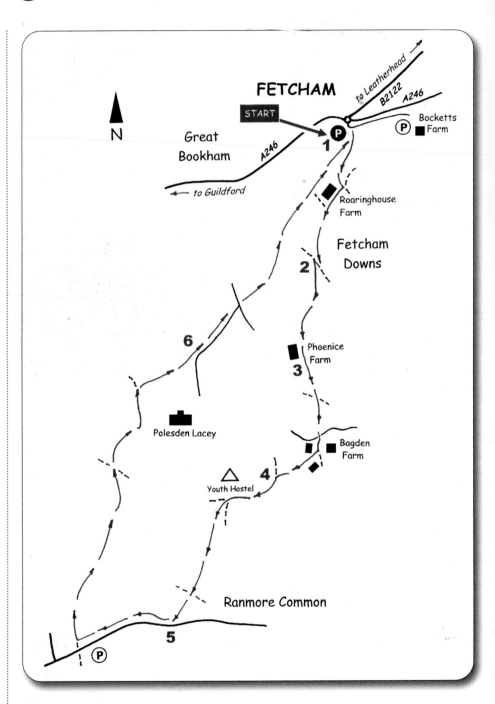

N

FETCHAM

START

to Leatherhead

B2122 A246

Bocketts Farm

1

Great Bookham

A246

to Guildford

Roaringhouse Farm

Fetcham Downs

2

Phoenice Farm

3

6

Polesden Lacey

Bagden Farm

4

Youth Hostel

Ranmore Common

5

■ *This ancient byway leads back towards Fetcham* ■

4 Turn left now on a rising bridleway that begins to climb the flank of the **North Downs**. The bridleway leads you past **Tanners Hatch Youth Hostel** where adventurous youngsters camp under the trees and gather around their fires at night. Immediately after passing the youth hostel, ignore a path ahead of you and turn left on a broader track for a few yards before forking right on a bridleway signed as **Belcham's Copse**. After zigzagging through woodland the track straightens and leads you to the top of the ridge and the road at **Ranmore Common**. Although the climb is reasonably easy, it is fairly long and will raise your heart rate and burn off many calories; don't overdo it and take a rest or two if necessary.
*Distance: 3.7 miles. **Guide time:** 1 hour 15 minutes.*

5 Having reached the top of the ridge our way is to the right, along a broad strip of grass keeping parallel to the road and ignoring enticing paths that lead back into the woodland. After ½ mile, pass **Ranmore car park** on the far side of the road and continue down a dip to meet a crossing byway.

■ *Tanners Hatch Youth Hostel* ■

Turn right here along the descending byway known as **Hogden Lane**. This good downhill section offers you the chance of increasing your pace and making up for any time lost during the climb. Ignore all side paths and remain on the well-marked byway (red arrows) as it passes through a shallow valley. Finally, after climbing a small rise and levelling out, the byway divides and here you should ignore the left fork and keep ahead. When a cart track enters from the right, remain ahead to meet the driveway to **Polesden Lacey House**.
*Distance: 6.26 miles. **Guide time:** 1 hour 55 minutes.*

6 Our way continues ahead along a wide grassy strip alongside the driveway where the views to London are quite stunning – from the Wembley arch in the west to skyscrapers glistening in the sun at Docklands in the east. When the driveway meets a small road junction, continue ahead along a byway known as **Admiral's Road**. From these heights you can now fill your lungs with fresh air, swing your arms and really get into your stride. Follow this great track for just over 1 mile until it ends at our outward path where a left turn brings you to the car park and the end of this exhilarating circuit.
*Distance: 8 miles. **Guide time:** 2 hours 30 minutes.*